NO DAMNS GIVEN

Who Has Time To Care About Sh*t That Don't Matter

Baker Robinson

Table of Contents

PART 1

Chapter 1:

Work Harder Than Everybody Else

Lacking motivation and lacking the drive and will to get up out of our butts to take that step towards making our dreams a reality is one that everyone struggles with, even me. Every single day, I wake up knowing the plan and the steps i need to take to get where I want to be, but i just can't seem to bring myself to do these necessary tasks. It is as if a wall is blocking my mind from wanting to do the work.

That is until i came across an article highlighting the power of just working harder than everybody else in whatever field or industry you are in. That you just work harder than your peers and success will come to you. And in this article, it tells the story of how Kobe Bryant, Jack Ma, Mark Cuban, and many other highly successful CEOs and entrepreneurs have achieved immense wealth and success just by working harder than anyone else.

While this concept may seem simple, it is certainty not as easy as it sounds. Putting hours more than your peers when they could be out there relaxing, enjoying life, partying and what not is a sacrifice that not everyone is willing to make. But it is this insane work ethic that drives these people to levels of success not seen by their peers.

Kobe Bryant puts this the best. With every 4 hours more that he practices more than his peers on the basketball court everyday, it starts to add up and compound in an incredible way that by the 5th year of training, none of his peers would ever be able to catch up to him no matter how hard they trained before every tournament or championship. By the time comes around, Kobe would have clocked in thousands of hours more than his peers in practice, and what he lacks for in talent (which I doubt is a factor), he makes up for in time on the court. And this time is what makes him one of the best players of all time. Putting him in the league of legends such as Michael Jordan.

The takeaway from Kobe's story is that every minute extra that you put in more than your peers will add up in time and put you leaps and bounds better than your competition. This can be applied to any field, whether it be a real estate career, as an investor, a trader, an athlete. Anything you set aside time for, you will gain the knowledge in time. You just have to start believing in the hours that you put in will pay off eventually.

This is a lesson that I have experienced personally as well. Many of us want to achieve happiness and success fast, today, now, but they forget that greatness isn't built in a day. And I realised that many of the things that i became good at took time to nurture. And the hours i put it only started paying off 2 to 3 years from the day I began embarking on that new journey or career. and I expect that my future endeavours will also take time to grow.

It is the same as watering a baby sprout everyday and giving it sunlight and water consistently, it only starts to grow really big by its 2nd or 3rd year being a healthy plant constantly fed with nutrients to ensure it has the best chance of survival and growth.

I challenge you today to work harder than everybody else around you and have an insane work ethic. Grind it out every single day, put in the hours that is necessary until you succeed and work your face off. Dont settle for anything less and remove distractions that suck out your time. If you outwork everyone every single day, you will eventually come out on top no matter how talented your competition might be. Just give it your best and never give up.

I hope you learned something today and are taking the necessary steps to get one step closed to your dreams. I wish you success and happiness. Take care and see you in the next one.

Chapter 2:

When It Is Time To Say No To Things

In my previous video I talked about the joys of saying yes to things and taking time out of your work to enjoy life and hanging out with friends. And I encouraged everyone to put themselves in favourable positions where they could say yes to things. However the question that we have to answer for ourselves today is "when should we draw the line and when does yes actually stops yielding benefits and instead could harm our progress towards the goals that we have set for ourselves?

To answer this question, I will bring it back to my own life once again to try and give it some perspective. As all of you know by now, I was working hard in prioritising social activities as I felt that there was a huge imbalance in my work life and my play life. At one point in my life, work was a full on 99% and play was a measly 1%. And simple math would tell you that it wasn't very healthy at all.

But as I started baking in more fun activities into my schedule, the percentage difference grew smaller and smaller. And it became so easy to simply choose fun over work that i actually started spending less time on my work than I did on friends. And similarly, simple math would tell u that too much of a good thing might not actually be that good after all.

As an entrepreneur, I am what I put into my business. And less time spent on my work also meant that I started falling behind on deadlines that I had set for myself at the beginning of the year. I became increasingly complacent and my income started to stagnate. It was at the point that i knew again that I needed to change something. I needed to tweak and prioritise my time more wisely. Carving time out for work whilst also balancing friends and sports for health and fitness purposes.

For those working a 9-5 job, there is a clear definition between work time and play time, but as as someone who is self employed, that line is often blurred. And without proper structure, commitment, and time management, one can easily fall into the trap of simply justifying time off. There is no boss breathing down my neck and that could be a good or bad thing depending on how you look at it.

You see, life is all about constant adjustments and fine tuning until we reach an equilibrium that we can say is the perfect balance. That ratio need not necessarily be 50/50, it could be any ratio that you decide it should be. I decided that I needed to spend 70% of my time on work at 30% of my time on social activities. And my next goal was to restructure my time accordingly. that meant that I needed to learn how to say no or grab a rain check when friends asked me out.

I also had to figure out what kind of work and play schedule would work for me. And the easiest was to look at my calender to carve out blocks of time that I know i would be the most productive and to just work as much as i could. If someone were to ask me out on those blocks of time, i needed to have the discipline to say no and to ask for a reschedule into one of the slots of that I have set aside for play.

You see I know myself better than anyone, and I know that if I scheduled play before work, 99% of the time, I would just end up spending the whole day playing and then regretting after that I had not done any work at all. So knowing yourself and how you function is key here in deciding when to say no or yes to things.

As I became more disciplined in saying no, I saw my productivity at work start to pic.   R   Rk up again. And I was back on track to reaching my goals again. I also slowly clawed my productivity back up to 70%. And I felt that it was the perfect balance for me.

So the takeaway from today's video is that you need to figure out what your goals are and exactly how much time you should or need to spend on your work to justify to yourselves that you have put in enough work to move the needle forward in your life without sacrificing time with friends. You need to be busy enough to be productive but not too busy that you come across as unavailable all the time. And you need to know who you are as a person and what exactly the balance is that you need to ensure that you are covering all areas of your life and that you are satisfied and happy with that decision.

So I challenge each and everyone of you today to take stock of your time, how you are spending them, what your goals are, so that when an invite comes, you know exactly whether to say no or yes without feelings of regret.

I hope you learned something new today and i wish you all the best in your endeavours. Take care and I'll see you in the next one.

Chapter 3:
The Struggle With Time

Today we're going to talk about a topic that isn't commonly looked at in depth. But it is one that we might hopefully find a new appreciation for. And that is TIME.

Time is a funny thing, we are never really aware of it and how much of a limited resource it really is until we get a rude awakening. Most commonly when our mortality is tested. Whether it be a health scare, an accident, a death of a loved one, a death of a pet, we always think we have more time before that. That we will always have time to say i love you, to put off the things we always told ourselves we needed to do, to start making that change, to spend time with the people that mean the most to us.

As we go about our days, weeks and months, being bothered and distracted by petty work, by our bosses, colleagues, trying to climb the corporate ladder, we forget to stop and check in on our fiends and family... We forget that their time may be running out, and that we may not have as much time with them as we think we do, until it is too late, and then we regret not prioritising them first. All the money that we made could not ever buy back the time we have lost with them. And that is something we have to live with if we ever let that happen.

The other funny thing about time is that if we don't set it aside for specific tasks, if we don't schedule anything, we will end up wasting it on something mindless. Whether it be browsing social media endlessly, or bingeing on television, we will never run out of things to fill that time with. Can you imagine that even though time is so precious, we willingly sacrifice and trade it in for self isolation in front of our TVs and computers for hours on end. Sometimes even for days? Or even on mobile games. Some being so addictive that it consumes most of our waking hours if we are not careful.

Our devices have become dangerous time wasters. It is a tool Shea its literally sapping the living energy out of us. Which is why some responsible companies have started implementing new features that help us keep track of our screen time. To keep us in check, and to not let our children get sucked into this black hole that we might struggle to climb out of.

I believe the biggest struggle with time that we all have is how to spend it in such a way that we can be happy without feeling guilty. Guilty of not spending it wisely. And I believe the best way to start is to start defining the things that you need to do, and the things that you want to do. And then striking a balance. To set equal amounts of time into each activity so that it doesn't overwhelm or underwhelm you. Spend one hour on each activity each day that you feel will have an impact on your life in a meaningful way, and you can spend your time on television or games without remorse.

So I challenge each of you to make the most of your time. SPending time with loved ones always come first, followed by your goals and dreams, and then leisure activities. Never the other way around. That way you can be at the end of your life knowing that you had not wasted the most precious commodity that we are only given a finite amount of. Money can't buy back your youth, your health, or time with loved ones, so don't waste it.

I believe in each and everyone of you, take care, and as always ill see you in the next one.

Chapter 4:

Showing Up

Today we are going to talk about the simple concept of "Showing Up".
And this is going to touch on the topic of motivation as well.

You see for many of us who struggle with laziness and a lack of willpower, we wait for inspiration to strike, or the perfect storm of feeling good and motivated before we make the effort to hit the hit or start taking action on the task that we have been putting off. We think that we need to be all pumped up and excited before doing anything, but many a times, these feelings are few and they rarely come when we expect them to.

There are days where I would plan a gym session only to cancel because I didn't feel like it. And there are times when I would plan a meetup with my friends only to feel lazy at the last second and cancelling. And there are also times when I plan to work at a particular cafe but decided against it because I was too tired.

All these moments where I lacked the willpower to get things started or keeping to my word only made my future commitments even more vulnerable to default. As i was giving in to my desires to be lazy, the next time it came around the excuses became easier and easier to justify. And that only led to a less favourable outcome with regards to my mental, physical, and emotional health. I was spiraling to a life of mediocrity every time i let my inner demon win.

This all changed when I came across an article that said that all you needed to do was to show up for your activity, even if u didn't want to. Just to do a quick 5 min session rather than a long 1 hour session that i would normally have planned out. Or to simply just get to the desk to work for 15mins rather than the 5 hours I would normally have set aside time to do.

I found that by the simple act of showing up for my activity, I had given myself the best possible chance to fulfilling that promise to myself. At the gym, one rep turned into 10 reps, and 5 mins of workout turned into a 2 hour one as i told myself you can do one more, and one more after that. And as I watched people workout around me, i felt motivated to put in more effort in my workout as well. This simple change made it easier for me to simply show up the next day at the gym and let the process play out on its own once again. The same principle came to work and play. I realised that all i needed to do was to get out of the house and the rest would take care of itself. To show up at my desk and gym, no matter how late I may be, that at least when I am there, I will begin the task one way or another.

I challenge each and everyone of you to give it a try. If you find the task that you dread to be too daunting, that Instead of setting a specific time that you need to spend on it, that you simply just show up. And let your body dictate how much time you should indeed spend on that activity. Be it 5 mins or 5 hours. I have found that once I start something that it takes a lot of energy for me to stop. It is like a moving train or car, that once u get going you will most probably go till you can't go no more. Then you slowly grind to a halt and show up for the next activity.

I hope you have learned something today and I wish you all the best in getting your stuff done ASAP. Take care and i'll see you in the next one.

Chapter 5:
Share Your Troubles Freely and Openly

Life is hard. We go through tons of challenges, problems, and obstacles every single day. We accumulate problems and stresses left right and Center. Absorbing each impact blow for blow.

Over time, these impacts will wear us down mentally and physically. Without a proper release channel, we find that our emotions spill over in ways when we least expect it. We get easily irritated, have a hard time falling asleep, have mood issues, and find ourselves even being temporarily depressed at times.

When we bottle negativity, it festers inside us without us realising what we have done. That is where releasing those tensions by pouring our heart and soul into friends, writing, journaling, and other outlets that allow us to express our feelings freely without judgement.

We may not all have friends that we can truly count on to share our deepest darkest secrets for fear that they might share these secrets unsuspectingly. If we do have these types of friends, treasure them and seek them out regularly to share your problems. By bouncing ideas off someone, we may even find a new solution to an old problem that we couldn't before. The other party may also be able to see things more objectively and with a unique perspective that is contrary to yours which you could potentially use to your advantage.

If writing things down is something that helps you cope with life, then by all means take a piece of paper and write down all the things that have been bothering you. Journal it, archive it. You may even write a song about it if that helps you process things better. Writing things down help us clear our minds and lets us see the big picture when we come back to it at a later date should we feel ready to address it. When things are too crazy, we may not have the mental capacity to handle everything being thrown at us at one go. So take the time to sort those feelings out.

You may also choose to just find a place that brings you relaxation. Whether it be going to the beach, or renting a hotel, or even just screaming at the top of your lungs. Let those feelings out. Don't keep it hidden inside.

IF all these things still don't work for you, you may want to try seeking help from a professional counsellor or therapist who can work out these issues you have in your life one by one. Never be afraid to book an appointment because your mental health is more important than the stigma associated with seeing a professional. You are not admitting you have a problem, you are simply acknowledge that there are areas in your life that you need assistance with. And that it is perfectly okay and perfectly normal to do so. Counsellors have the passion to serve, the passion to help, and that is why they chose that profession to being with. So seek their assistance and guidance as much as you need to.

Life isn't easy. But we can all take a conscious effort to regulate our emotions more healthily to live a long and balanced life.

Chapter 6:

Overcoming Your Fears

Today we're going to talk about the topic of fears. What fear is and how we can overcome it. Now before we dive into it, let us just take a brief moment to think of or right down what our greatest fears are right now.

Whether it be taking the next step in your relationship, fear of the unknown, fear of quitting your job and not finding another one, fear or death, fear of illnesses, whatever fear that jumps out at you and is just eating at you at the back of your mind, i want you to remember that fear as we go through this video.

So what is fear exactly? Whilst there are many definitions of fear out there, I'm going to take, as usual, my spin on things. And to me fear is simply a negative feeling that you assign to usually a task that you really don't want to do. And most of the time, the fear is of the unknown, that you can't visualise what is going to happen next. You don't know whether the outcome will be good or bad, and you don't know whether it is the right move to make. So this trio of thoughts keep circling round and round and eventually you just decide that you are not going to take any action on it and you just shove it to one side hoping that it goes away. And whilst you may do that temporarily, sometimes even for months, one day you are going to have to come face to face with it again. And when that day comes, you will either be paralysed again or you may again put it off to a later date.

We procrastinate on our fears because we want a sure thing. We want to know what will happen next, and we fear what we don't know.

Now for the fears that we are talking about today, it is something that will affect your life if u don't take action. If it is like a fear of bungee jumping or sky driving, sure that fear is physical and very real, but also you can make a choice not to do it and your problem is solved. It will not affect your life in a negative way if u don't do it.

But if it is a fear of a career switch because you already hate your job so much and are totally miserable, that is a fear that you should do your best to try and address as soon as possible.

So what can and should you do about these sorts of fears? The answer for this one is not going to be that difficult. Simply think of the consequences of not conquering your task and how much it might prevent you from moving forward in life and you have got your answer.

When the pain associated with not accomplishing the task becomes greater than the fear we assign to it, it is the tipping point that we need to finally take that action. But instead of waiting to get to that excruciating pain, we can visualise and project what it could potentially feel like if we don't do it now and the pain we might feel at a later day, say 1 year from now, when we have wasted another full year of our life not taking that leap of faith, the time we have burned, the time we can never get back, and the opportunity cost of not taking action now, we might just decide that we don;t want to wait until that day comes and face that huge amount of regret that we should've done something a lot sooner.

And what we need to simply do is to just take action. Taking action is something you will hear from all the gurus you will find out there. When faced with a fear or challenge, instead of wondering what dangers lurk in the unknown, just take action and let the experience tell you whether it was indeed the right or wrong decision. Do you necessary homework and due diligence beforehand and take that calculated step forward instead of procrastinating on it. Life is too short to be mucking around. Just go for it and never live your life in fear or regret ever again.

I challenge each and everyone of you to go through the list that we have created at the start of the video. The one that you have been most fearful of doing. And i want you to assess the pros and cons of each fear that you have written down. If there are more pros than cons, i want you to set a deadline for yourself that you will take action on it. And that deadline is today. Don't waste precious time worrying and instead spend more time doing.

I hope you learned something today and as always take care and i wish you all the best in overcoming your fears and achieving your goals as fast as possible. See you in the next one.

Chapter 7:

The Magic of Journaling

Today we're going to talk about the power of journaling, and why you should start making it as part of your daily habit starting today.

Everyday, every second of our lives, we are bombarded with things coming at our way. From our colleagues, our bosses, to our friends, families, relationships, and most importantly, ourselves. Life gets hectic and crazy sometimes. We have a million things racing through our minds and we don't have the time or place to let it all out so we keep it bottled up inside.

This creates a backlog of emotions, feelings, things, that we leave un-dealt with. We start to miss the little details along the way, or our mood gets affected because we can't seem to get rid of the negativity festering up inside of us. If we don't have anyone readily available to talk to us, these feelings that have been building inside of us could end up spilling over and affecting our performance at the workplace, at home, whatever it may be.

We are not able to perform these roles at home or at work effectively as a result. This is where the power of journaling comes into play.

Journaling is such an important tool for us to put into paper or into words every single emotion that we are feeling. Every thought that we are thinking. And this works sort of like a cleanse. We are cleansing, decluttering, and unpacking all the things that are jumbled up in our head. By writing these feelings down, we are not only able to keep a clear head, but it also gives us a reference point to come back to if there are any unresolved problems that we feel we need to work on at a later date.

Journaling has worked wonders for me. I've never thought it to be a habit work incorporating into my life because i thought hey, it's another thing for me to do on top of my already hectic day. I don't have time for this. Basically giving 1001 reasons not to do it.

But I came across this life coach that described the wonders of journaling as I am describing to you right now. And I thought. Why not just give it a try.

I did. And it changed my life.

I never realized how powerful journaling could actually be in transforming my state of mind and to always keep me grounded and focused. Everytime I felt that i was distracted, had something I couldn't work through in my mind, I would pick up my ipad and start typing it down in a journal app.

With technology, it has made journaling a much more enjoyable experience for me and one that i can simply do on the fly, anywhere, anytime. I didn't have to fumble around to find my pen and book, i just opened up the app and started typing away every single feeling and thought.

Journaling helped me see the big picture. It helped me become more aware of the things that are working for me and things that aren't. I was able to focus more on the areas that were bringing more joy in my life and to eliminate the situations and activities that were draining me of my energy and spirit.

Journaling can be anything you want it to be. There are no fixed rules as to how you must journal. Just write whatever comes to your mind. You will be surprised by how much you can learn from yourself. Many a times we forget that we are our best teacher. Other people can't learn our lessons for us, only we can.

So next time you feel sluggish, depressed, unhappy, or even ecstatic and over the moon, write down how and why you got to that place. No judgement, no berating yourself, just pouring your heart and soul onto a piece of paper or into a journaling app. I'll be looking forward to hearing of your transformation from the power of journaling.

Structure Your Day With Tasks You Excel At and Enjoy

Today's video will probably appeal to people who have a say in the way they can structure their day. People who are working on their own businesses, or are freelancers. But it could also apply to those with full time jobs if your jobs allow flexibility.

For those who have been doing their own thing for a while, we know that it is not easy to put together a day that is truly enjoyable. We forget about doing the things we like and excel at, and start getting lost in a sea of work that we have to drag ourselves through doing.

If we don't have a choice, then I guess we can't really do anything about it. But if we do, we need to start identifying the tasks that require the most attention but the least effort on our part to do. Tasks that seem just about second-nature to us. Tasks that we would do even if nobody wanted to pay us. Tasks that allow our creativity to grow and expand, tasks that challenge us but not drain us, tasks that enriches us, or tasks that we simply enjoy doing.

The founding father of modern Singapore, one of the wealthiest countries in the world, Mr Lee Kuan Yew once said, find what works and just keep doing it over and over again. I would apply that to this situation as well. We have to find what works for us and just double down on it. The other stuff that we aren't good at, either hire someone else to do it, or find a way to do less of it or learn how to be good at it fast. Make it a challenge for ourselves. Who knows maybe you might find them enjoyable once you get a hang of it as well.

But for those things that already come naturally to us, do more of it. Pack a lot of time into at the start of the day. Dedicated a few hours of your day to those meaningful tasks that you excel at. You will find that once you get the creative juices and the momentum going, you will be able to conquer the other less pleasing tasks more easily knowing that you've already accomplished your goals for the day.

Start right now. Identify what those tasks that you absolutely love to do right now, work-wise, or whatever it may be, and just double down on it. Watch your day transform.

Chapter 8:

Planning Ahead

The topic that are going to discuss today is probably one that is probably not going to apply to everybody, especially for those who have already settled down with a house, wife, kids, a stable career, and so on. But i still believe that we can all still learn something from it. And that is to think about planning ahead. Or rather, thinking long term.

You see, for the majority of us, we are trained to see maybe 1 to 2 years ahead in our lives. Being trained to do so in school, we tend to look towards our next grade, one year at a time. And this system has ingrained in us that we find it hard to see what might and could happen 2 or 3 years down the road.

Whilst there is nothing wrong with living life one year at a time, we tend to fall into a short term view of what we can achieve. We tell ourselves we must learn a new instrument within 1 year and be great at it, or we must get this job in one year and become the head of department, or we must find our partner and get married within a short amount of time. However, life does not really work that way, and things actually do take much longer, and we do actually need more time to grow these small little shoots into big trees.

We fail to see that we might have to give ourselves a longer runway time of maybe 3-5 or even 10 years before we can become masters in a new instrument, job, relationship, or even friendships. Rome isn't built in a day and we shouldn't expect to see results if we only allow ourselves 1 year to accomplish those tasks. Giving ourselves only 1 year to achieve the things we want can put unnecessary pressure on ourselves to expect results fast, when in reality no matter how much you think u think rushing can help you achieve results faster, you might end up burning yourself out instead.

For those short term planners, even myself. I have felt that at many stages in my life, i struggle to see the big picture. I struggle to see how much i can achieve in lets say 5 years if i only allowed myself that amount of time to become a master in whatever challenge i decide to take on. Even the greatest athletes take a longer term view to their career. They believe that if they practice hard each day, they might not expect to see results in the first year, but as their efforts compound, by the 5th year they would have already done so much practice that it is statistically impossible not to be good at it.

And when many of us fall into the trap of simply planning short term, our body reacts by trying to rush the process as well. We expect everything to be fast fast fast, and results to be now now now. And we set unrealistic goals that we cannot achieve and we beat ourselves up for it come December 31st.

Instead i believe many of us should plan ahead by giving ourselves a minimum of 2.5 years in whatever task we set to achieve, be it an income goal, a fitness goal, or a relationship goal. 2.5 years is definitely much more manageable and it gives us enough room to breathe so that we don't stress ourselves out unnecessarily. If you feel like being kinder to yourself, you might even give yourselves up to 5 years. And again the key to achieving success with proper long term planning is Consistency. If you haven't watched my video on consistency do check it out as i believe it is one of the most important videos that I have ever created.

I believe that with a run time of 5 years and consistency in putting the hours every single day, whether it is an hour or 10 hours, that by the end of it, there is no goal that you cannot achieve. And we should play an even longer game of 10 years or so. Because many of the changes we want to make in life should be permanent and sustainable. Not a one off thing. So I challenge each and everyone of you today to not only plan ahead, but to think ahead of the longevity of the path that you have set for yourself. There is no point rushing through life and missing all the incredible sights along the way. I am sure you will be a much happier person for it.

I hope you learned something today, take care and I'll see you in the next one.

The Power of Imperfect Starts

When you have a goal — starting a business or eating healthier, or traveling the world — it's easy to look at someone who is already doing it and then try to reverse engineer their strategy. In some cases, this is useful. Learning from the experiences of successful people is a great way to accelerate your learning curve.

But it's equally important to remember that the systems, habits, and strategies that successful people are using today are probably not the same ones they were using when they began their journey. What is optimal for them right now isn't necessarily needed for you to get started. There is a difference between the two.

Let me explain.

What is Optimal vs. What is Needed

Learning from others is great, and I do it all the time myself.

But comparing your current situation to someone already successful can often make you feel like you lack the required resources to get started at all. If you look at their optimal setup, it can be really easy to convince yourself that you need to buy new things or learn new skills or meet new people before you can even take the first step toward your goals.

And usually, that's not true. Here are two examples.

Starting a business. When you're an entrepreneur, it's so easy to get obsessed with optimal. This is especially true at the start. I can remember being convinced that my first website would not succeed without a great logo. After all, every popular website I looked at had a professional logo.

I've since learned my lesson. Now my "logo" is just my name, and this is the most popular website I've built.

Eating healthy. Maybe the optimal diet would involve buying beef that is only grass-fed or vegetables that are only organic, or some other super-healthy food strategy. But if you're just trying to make strides in the right direction, why get bogged down in the details? Start small and simply buy another vegetable this week — whether it's organic or not. There will be plenty of time for optimization later.

Avoiding by Optimizing

Claiming that you need to "learn more" or "get all of your ducks in a row" can often be a crutch that prevents you from moving forward on the stuff that matters.

- You can complain that your golf game is suffering because you need new clubs, but the truth is you probably just need two years of practice.

- You can point out how your business mentor is successful because they use XYZ software, but they probably got started without it.

Obsessing about the ultimate strategy, diet, or golf club can be a clever way to prevent yourself from doing hard work.

An imperfect start can always be improved, but obsessing over a perfect plan will never take you anywhere on its own.

Chapter 9:

Understanding Yourself

Today we're going to talk about a topic that hopefully helps you become more aware of who you are as a person. And why do you exist right here and right now on this Earth. Because if we don't know who we are, if we don't understand ourselves, then how can we expect to other stand and relate to others? And why we even matter?

How many of you think that you can describe yourself accurately? If someone were to ask you exactly who you are, what would you say? Most of us would say we are Teachers, doctors, lawyers, etc. We would associate our lives with our profession.

But is that really what we are really all about?

Today I want to ask you not what you do, and not let your career define you, but rather what makes you feel truly alive and connected with the world? What is it about your profession that made you want to dedicated your life and time to it? Is there something about the job that makes you want to get up everyday and show up for the work, or is it merely to collect the paycheck at the end of the month?

I believe that that there is something in each and everyone of us that makes us who we are, and keeps us truly alive and full. For those that dedicate their lives to be Teachers, maybe they see themselves as an educator, a role model, a person who is in charge of helping a kid grow up, a nurturer, a parental figure. For Doctors, maybe they see themselves as healers, as someone who feels passionate about bringing life to someone. Whatever it may be, there is more to them than their careers.

For me, I see myself as a future caregiver, and to enrich the lives of my family members. That is something that I feel is one of my purpose in life. That I was born, not to provide for my family monetary per se, but to provide the care and support for them in their old age. That is one of my primary objectives. Otherwise, I see and understand myself as a person who loves to share knowledge with others, as I am doing right now. I love to help others in some way of form, either to inspire them, to lift their spirits, or to just be there for them when they need a crying shoulder. I love to help others fulfill their greatest potential, and it fills my heart with joy knowing that someone has benefitted from my advice. From what I have to say. And that what i have to say actually does hold some merit, some substance, and it is helping the lives of someone out there.. to help them make better decisions, and to help the, realise that life is truly wonderful. That is who i am.

Whenever I try to do something outside of that sphere, when what I do does not help someone in some way or another, I feel a sense of dread. I feel that what I do becomes misaligned with my calling, and I drag my feet each day to get those tasks done. That is something that I have realized about myself. And it might be happening to you too.

If u do not know exactly who you are and why you are here on this Earth, i highly encourage you to take the time to go on a self-discovery journey, however long it may take, to figure that out. Only when you know exactly who you are, can you start doing the work that aligns with ur purpose and calling. I don't meant this is in a religious way, but i believe that each and every one of us are here for a reason, whether it may to serve others, to help your fellow human beings, or to share your talents with the world, we should all be doing something with our lives that is at least close to that, if not exactly that.

So I challenge each and everyone of you to take this seriously because I believe you will be much happier for it. Start aligning your work with your purpose and you will find that life is truly worth living.

Chapter 10:

Trust The Process

Today we're going to talk about the power of having faith that things will work out for you even though you can't see the end in sight just yet. And why you need to simply trust in the process in all the things that you do.

Fear is something that we all have. We fear that if we quit our jobs to pursue our passions, that we may not be able to feed ourselves if our dreams do not work out. We fear that if we embark on a new business venture, that it might fail and we would have incurred financial and professional setbacks.

All this is borne out of the fear of the unknown. The truth is that we really do not know what can or will happen. We may try to imagine in our heads as much as we can, but we can never really know until we try and experienced it for ourselves.

The only way to overcome the fear of the unknown is to take small steps, one day at a time. We will, to the best of our ability, execute the plan that we have set for ourselves. And the rest we leave it up to the confidence that our actions will lead to results.

If problems arise, we deal with it there and then. We put out fires, we implement updated strategies, and we keep going. We keep going until we have exhausted all avenues. Until there is no more roads for us to travel, no more paths for us to create. That is the best thing that we can do.

If we constantly focus on the fear, we will never go anywhere. If we constantly worry about the future, we will never be happy with the present. If we dwell on our past failures, we will be a victim of our own shortcomings. We will not grow, we will not learn, we will not get better.

I challenge each and every one of you today to make the best out of every situation that you will face. Grab fear by the horns and toss them aside as if it were nothing. I believe in you and all that you can achieve.

7 Ways To Know If You're A Good Person

This question is something that we wonder from time to time. When we are at our lowest point and we look around, there could be a chance that there may not be that many people in our lives that we can really count on.

We start to wonder how people actually see us. Are we good people? Have we been nice to those around us? Or do we come off as pretentious and hence people tend to stay clear of us for some reason.

There is a dilemma lately about the use of social media and having followers. It seems that people are interested in following your socials, but when it comes to you asking them out or chatting them up, they don't respond or are uninterested to meet up with you.

You then start to wonder if there is something wrong with you. You start to question your morals, your self-worth, and everything about your life. This can quickly spiral out of control and lead to feelings that you are somehow flawed.

Today we're going to help you answer that question: Am I a good person? Here are 7 Ways To Find Out If You Are Indeed One

1.   Look At The People Who Have Stuck Around

I think this one is a good place to start for all of us. Instead of wondering if we have gone wrong somewhere, take a look at the friends and family who have stuck around for you over all this time. They are still there for you for a reason. You must have done something right for them not to leave you for other people. Sure some of them may not be as close as they once were, but they are still there. Think about the people who celebrate your birthdays with you, the people who still asks if you want to hang out from time to time, and the people who you can count on in times of emergency. We may not be able to determine if we are good people from this, but we know that at least we are not so far off the rails.

2.   Ask Them To Be Honest With You

If you really want to find out if you are a good person, ask your friends directly and honestly, to point out to you areas that they feel you need to work on. Sometimes we cannot see the flaws and the misguided actions that we portray to the world. People may gradually dislike and drift away from us quietly without telling us why. The people who have stuck around know you best, so let them be brutally honest with you. Take what they have to say as constructive criticism, rather than a personal attack on your character. It is better to know in what areas you lack as a person and to work to improve it, than to go through life obliviously and thinking that there is absolutely nothing wrong with you.

3. Think About Why Your Friends May Not Respond To Your
    Messages

Many a times friendships simply run its natural course. As work, relationships, and family come into the picture, it is inevitable that people drift apart over time. If you decide to hit your friends up and they don't respond, don't take it too personally. It could be that maybe you're just not a vital piece of the puzzle in their lives anymore. If their friendships aren't one that you have been cultivating anyway, you may want to consider removing them completely from your lives. Find new people who will appreciate and love you rather than dwell on the past. There may be nothing wrong with you as a person, it's just the cruel nature of time playing its dirty game.

4. Keeping It Real With Yourself

Do you think that you are a good person? The fact that you are here shows that you may already have an inclination that something may not be quite right with you but you can't quite put a finger on it. Instead of looking for confirmation from external sources, try looking within. Ask yourself the hard questions. Think about every aspect of your life and evaluate yourself. If you have more enemies than friends, maybe there is something you aren't doing quite right that needs some work. Write those possible flaws down and see if you can work through them.

5. Do You Try Your Best To Help Others?

Sometimes we may not be great friends but we may be great at other things, such as being passionate about a cause or helping other people. Maybe friendships aren't a priority for us and hence it is not a good indicator of whether we are good people by looking at the quality of our friendships. If instead we are driven by a cause bigger than ourselves, and we participate through volunteering, events, and donation drives, we can pat ourselves on the back and say that at least we have done something meaningful to better the lives of others. In my opinion you are already a winner.

6. Is Life Always About What You Want?

This one could be a red flag because if we create a life that is only centred around us, we are in danger of being self-obsessive. Having the "Me First" attitude isn't something to be proud of. Life is about give and take, and decisions should be made fairly for all parties involved. If you only want to do things your way, or go to places you want, at the expense of the opinions of others, you are driving people away without realising it. Nobody likes someone who only thinks about themselves. If you catch yourself in this position, it may be time to consider a 180 turn.

7. People Enjoy Being Around You

While this may not be the best indicator that you are a good person, it is still a decent way to tell if you are well-liked and if people enjoy your presence. Generally people are attracted to others who are kind, loyal, trustworthy, and charismatic. If people choose to ask you out, they could find you to be one of those things, which is a good sign that you're not all too bad. Of course you could have ulterior motives for presenting yourself in a well-liked manner, but disingenuity usually gets found out eventually and you very well know if you are being deceitful to others for your own personal gain.

Conclusion

There is no sure-fire way to tell if you are a good person. No one point can be definitive. But you can definitely look at a combination of factors to determine the possibility of that age-old question. The only thing you can do is to constantly work on improving yourself. Invest time and effort into becoming a better person and never stop striving for growth in your character.

No Damns Given

PART 2

Chapter 1:

The Power of Community

The topic that we are going to discuss today is something that I feel has resonated with me one a more personal level recently. And it is one that I have largely neglected in the past.

As i have mentioned before in other videos, that as an entrepreneur of sorts, my job required me to work independently, mostly from home. And while it may sound nice to others, or even yourself, where you think it is a privilege to work from home, many a times it is actually not all that fun because there is no sense of community or interaction with others. And the job becomes quite lonesome.

I'm sure many of you who have experienced lockdowns and Work from home situations, that it may seem fun for a week, but after that you realize that actually it isn't all that it is cracked out to be. And you actually do wanna get dressed, get out of the house, and go somewhere to do your work rather than stay in your PJs all day and waste your time away.

But if you dig deeper, you will realize that what you actually miss is the interaction with your co-workers, to just walk over to their desk to ask them something, or simply to just start a conversation because maybe you're bored, or to have lunch together instead of cooking your own instant noodles at home.

As social creatures, we crave that human interaction. And we crave belonging in a community and being a part of something bigger than ourselves.

When we are in lockdown, we lose that personal touch that we have with others, and we start to feel restless, we feel that something is missing but we can't put our finger on it. It is not the actual work at the job that we look forward to, but rather the people, the colleagues that make working fun and enjoyable.

The same goes for any sports of workout. You will realize that when you gym alone, you are less likely to show up because there is no one there to push you to make you do one more rep. There is no community to keep you going back to stick to your goals. For those of you who do yoga, i am sure the experience is very different when you practice an hour of yoga at home versus in a yoga studio with 30 other people, even if you don't know any of them. There is still a sense that you are a part of a greater unit, a class that works out together, a group of like-minded individuals who really want the same thing and share the same interests. You feel compelled to go back because the community is there to make the exercise fun. That after a tiring workout you look to the people beside and around you and you see the same expressions on their faces. That they had shared an activity with you and feel the same things. Isn't that what life is really about? To be a part of something rather than going about it like a lone wolf?

So for those of you who feel like something is amiss in the activity that you once loved, be it a sports or a job, or an activity that you have no choice to do but never felt happy doing it, i challenge you to find a like-minded community who share the same beliefs and interests. You can easily look for such groups on meet-up apps. You might find that the missing puzzle is indeed other individuals that share your likes. And when you work around them or with them, you will feel a much greater sense of joy and happiness that you never thought you could feel.

I hope you learned something today and I'll see you in the next one. Take care.

Chapter 2:

Put Yourself In Positions of Opportunity

Today I examined a story of a very famous woman in Singapore who had a less than perfect childhood, but grew up to become a big personality in the media industry. The woman I am fascinated today is the artiste known as Sharon Au.

You see, Sharon was a child of divorced parents. She moved from home to home, staying with relatives up until she was 17. Her parents were never really there for her but she had something special in her. She was resilient and she always strived to be the best.

While she did not intend to be a famous personality, she auditioned for a role as a dancer in a musical after having seen it many times before on stage, learning the songs word for word. This immediately impressed the auditioner who casted her the role of the lead.

Now we have our first example of how she had placed herself in a position of opportunity and got herself a start in what would be a lucrative career as a media personnel. The first takeaway is that she dared to try. She dared to audition. And she dared to challenge herself to be placed in a role where she could further showcase her talents. This was her at age 20.

With this first opened door, she and her cast in the musical managed to sell out 16 shows. And as luck would have it once again, she made a remarkable performance on one of the show nights while a big head of a media executive company was there to watch. She was offered a contract immediately and from there her media career took off.

She subsequently appeared in countless tv shows and became a prominent tv personality in the Singapore media industry. As her fame and popularity escalated, so did the number of opportunities in the form of contracts and endorsements that followed. She subsequently became so popular that she won numerous awards and accolades for her performance as a host and actress.

After spending more than 10 years in the media industry, she decided to pursue her initial dream of going to university at age 30. She left her lucrative entertainment career in Singapore for a university in Japan and appeared on the deans list multiple times while impressively studying and completing her education in a foreign language. She is now currently a investment director working in Paris.

I just want to impress on you today on how one decision in her life, to audition for a role in a musical, let to a chain of events that brought her much successes in her very fulfilling yet ever changing career in work and life. She had effectively placed herself in a position of opportunity one time which had led to multiple opportunities and doors opening for her like a floodgate. Barring her talent and tireless work ethic that should inspire everyone should you dig deeper into her life and career, she remains a gem in Singapore's history as an icon who had left a mark on the entertainment history even till this day.

I want to challenge all of you to not give up in placing yourself in areas where opportunities can present themselves to you. You might not know when or how it might hit you, but when it does, it can come so fast and so great that you better be prepared for it.

I hope you all enjoyed the sharing today and i hope you learned something new to improve your life and situation. As always see you in the next one.

Chapter 3:

Overcoming Fear and Self-Doubt

The lack of belief most people have is the reason for their failure at even the smallest things in life. The biggest killer of dreams is the lack of belief in ourselves and the doubt of failure.

We all make mistakes. We all have some ghosts of the past that haunt us. We all have something to hide. We all have something that we regret. But what you are today is not the result of your mistakes.

You are here because of your struggles to make those things go away. You are here now with the power and strength to shape your present and your future.

Our mind is designed to take the shape of what we hold long enough inside it. The things we frequently think about ultimately start filling in the spaces within our memory, so we have to be careful. We have to decide whether we want to stay happy or to hold on to the fear we once wanted to get rid of.

The human spirit and human soul are colored by the impressions we ourselves decide to impose.

The reason why we don't want to explore the possibility of what to do is that subconsciously we don't believe that it can happen for us. We don't believe that we deserve it or if it was meant for us.

So here is something I suggest. Ask yourself, how much time in a day do you spend thinking about your dream? How much time do you spend working on your dreams everyday? What books did you read this year? What new skills have you acquired recently? What have you done that makes you worthy of your dream? Nothing?

Then you are on point with your doubt because you don't have anything to show for when the opportunity presents itself.

You don't succeed because you have this latent fear. Fear that makes you think about the consequences of what will happen if you fail even with all the good things on your hand?

I know that feeling but failure is there to teach you one important and maybe the most essential skill life can teach us; Resilience.

You rediscover your life once you have the strength to fight your every fear and every doubt because you have better things on your hand to care for.

You have another dream to pursue. Another horizon awaits you. Another peak to summit. It doesn't matter if you literally have to run to stand still. You got to do what you got to do, no matter the consequences and the sacrifices.

But failing to do what is required of you has no justifiable defense. Not even fear. Because your fears are self-imposed and you already have many wrong things going on for you right now.

Don't let fear be one of them. Because fear is the most subtle and destructive disease So inhale all your positive energies and exhale all your doubts because you certainly are a better person without them.

Chapter 4:

Things That Spark Joy

I'm sure you've heard the term "spark joy", and this is our topic of discussion today that I am going to borrow heavily from Marie Kondo.

Now why do I find the term spark joy so fascinating and why have i used it extensively in all areas of my life ever since coming across that term a few years ago?

When I first watched Marie Kondo's show on Netflix and also reading articles on how this simple concept that she has created has helped people declutter their homes by choosing the items that bring joy to them and discarding or giving away the ones that don't, I began my own process of decluttering my house of junk from clothes to props to ornaments, and even to furniture.

I realised that many things that looked good or are the most aesthetically pleasing, aren't always the most comfortable to use or wear. And when they are not my go to choice, they tend to sit on shelves collecting dust and taking up precious space in my house. And after going through my things one by one, this recurring theme kept propping up time and again. And i subconsciously associated comfort and ease of use with things that spark joy to me. If I could pick something up easily without hesitation to use or wear, they tend to me things that I gravitated to naturally, and these things began to spark joy when i used them. And when i started getting rid of things that I don't find particularly pleased to use, i felt my house was only filled with enjoyable things that I not only enjoyed looking at, but also using on a regular and frequent basis.

This association of comfort and ease of use became my life philosophy. It didn't apply to simply just decluttering my home, but also applied to the process of acquiring in the form of shopping. Every time i would pick something up and consider if it was worthy of a purpose, i would examine whether this thing would be something that I felt was comfortable and that i could see myself utilising, and if that answer was no, i would put them down and never consider them again because i knew deep down that it would not spark joy in me as I have associated joy with comfort.

This simple philosophy has helped saved me thousands of dollars in frivolous spending that was a trademark of my old self. I would buy things on the fly without much consideration and most often they would end up as white elephants in my closet or cupboard.

To me, things that spark joy can apply to work, friends, and relationships as well. Expanding on the act of decluttering put forth by Marie Kondo. If the things you do, and the people you hang out with don't spark you much joy, then why bother? You would be better off spending time doing things with people that you actually find fun and not waste everybody's time in the process. I believe you would also come out of it being a much happier person rather than forcing yourself to be around people and situations that bring you grief.

Now that is not to say that you shouldn't challenge yourself and put yourself out there. But rather it is to give you a chance to assess the things you do around you and to train yourself to do things that really spark joy in you that it becomes second nature. It is like being fine tuned to your 6th sense in a way because ultimately we all know what we truly like and dislike, however we choose to ignore these feelings and that costs us time effort and money.

So today's challenge is for you to take a look at your life, your home, your friendships, career, and your relationships. Ask yourself, does this thing spark joy? If it doesn't, maybe you should consider a decluttering of sorts from all these different areas in your life and to streamline it to a more minimalist one that you can be proud of owning each and every piece.

Take care and I'll see you in the next one.

Chapter 5:

Stay Focused

A razor sharp focus is required to bridge the gap
between our vision and our current circumstances.
Stay focused on the vision we want,
despite the current reality.
It's challenging to believe you will be rich when you are poor,
healthy if you are sick,
but it is necessary to achieve that vision.

Focus on the desired result.
Focus on the next step towards that goal.
Without focus on these elements there can be no success.
Stay focused on the positive elements,
solutions over problems.

The expected reward over the fear, loss and pain along the way.
What we focus on will become.
Therefore we have to maintain our eyes on the prize.

Be results driven.
Always focus on bringing that result closer.
Focus on what your grateful for.
Gratefulness brings more of that into your life.
Focus on problems on the other hand brings more problems.

If we focus on a big goal today,
we might not be ready yet,

but we will become ready on the way.

Commit to the necessary changes you know you need.
Get ourselves ready for that goal.
So many never act simply because they don't know how.
They don't feel ready.
We can achieve nearly anything if we focus on it.

Think carefully about what you focus on.
It is critical to both your success and failure.
Know exactly what you want.
See the odds of a successful happy life increase by unfathomable amounts.

How can we be happy and successful if we never define what that is?
It's not about what you are, or what you were in the past.
It is all about what you are becoming and want to become.

We cannot let circumstances or the world decide that.
We must use our free will and decide who and what we will become and focus fully on
that.
Wishing, succumbing to the days whim, will never bring lasting success.
Success requires serious commitment and focus on that outcome.
Exude a fanatical level of focus.
Be exuberated in the pursuit of success.

The most successful often focus on work for over 100 hours per week.
They give up most social interaction and even sleep to make that dream happen.
They do not find this hard or stressful because they are pursuing something they enjoy.

Focus on something you enjoy.
Stop spending your time and energy on a job that you hate.
Work in an area you enjoy.

It makes focusing and achieving success easier.

Keep in mind that your time is limited.
Is what you're doing right now moving you towards your goal?
If not stop.

It is crucial that you enjoy your journey.
Start planning some leisure time into your days.
The goal is to remain balanced while you stick to your schedule.

If you focus on nothing, you will receive nothing.
If you do nothing, you will become nothing.

Your focus is everything.
Get specific with your focus to steer your ships in the direction of the solid fertile land you desire.
Aim higher as you focus on bigger and better things.

Why focus on plan b if you believe in plan a?
Why not give all your focus to that?

Stay focused on the best result regardless of the perceived situation.
The world is pliable.
It will mould and change around you based on your thoughts and what you focus on.
Your free will means you are free to focus on what you want and ignore what you don't.

Focus on a future of greatness.
A future where you are healthy, happy, and wealthy.
See the limits as imaginary and watch them break down before you.
Understand that you are powerful and what you think matters in your life.

Become who you want to be,

Not who others think you should be.

This shift is one of the quickest roads to happiness.

When you focus on what you love,

You draw more of it into our lives.

You will become happier.

You must focus on a future that makes you and your family happy.

You must stay steadfast with an unwavering faith and focus on that result.

Because with faith and focus anything is possible.

Chapter 6:

Only Buying Things that serve a purpose For you

Today I'm going to talk about the right way to buy things. The right way to shop. The right way to spend your hard earned money.

You see, many of us think that we need to buy things to make working hard at our jobs worth the effort. Sure it does help, in the form of retail therapy for some, but a lot of times we end up just excessively buying things that clutter up our house, our space, our homes. Stuff that we only use once and never touch again. Clothes is a common way that this kind of hoarding happens. We don't notice it because we are buying one shirt or one pants at a time, but over just a few shopping sprees and we find our closets full to the brim. And we never wear some of these clothing's more than once, but we throw the "old" ones to make way for the new.

I believe that the right way to buy things is only to purchase quality items that truly deserve a spot in our homes. Things that bring us joy. Things that we are 1000% sure we will use regularly.

For me, I love apple products. I admit that this one area is where I spend most of my money. I may not buy clothes, shoes, bags, but i will definitely put down money to buy apple products. The thing though is that I only buy items that serve a purpose for me in everyday things that I do. As a music lover, i loved their audio products and the ease of which I can enjoy my favourite music and tv shows with their devices. And I use these products on a daily basis. Everytime i pick up an apple product, i find it such a joy to use.

If you get that same feeling with a particular item, it is okay to get it. I'm not here to tell you u shouldnt be buying anything. As long as it is within your means and you know it will not end up untouched for months, then by all means get it. If something doesn't serve you anymore, sell it, donate it away, keep your space free of clutter.

A clutter-free home can provide enormous benefits for our mental and emotional health. To quote Marie Kondo, and to go one step further, only buy things that truly spark joy in you. Never buy things just because. You may feel good in the moment to splurge, but that feeling won't last. Pick your battles and pick your items carefully.

Who Are You Working For?

Who you work for is up to you,
but ultimately every person has a choice in that decision.
Whether you are self-employed, self-made, or salaried,
You determine your own destiny.
As Earl Nightingale said, only the successful will admit it.

You might work for one company your whole life,
but ultimately you are still working for yourself and your family.
If you do not like the practices of your company,
you have the power to leave and make a change.
You must choose to serve who you believe to be worthy of your life.

High self-esteem stops successful people ever feeling subordinate to anyone.
Achieve your goals by envisioning yourself providing quality service in the companies
and places that will maximise your chances of success.

Always view yourself as equal to everybody.

All of us have unique talents and qualities within us.

Acknowledg that we can learn from anybody.

Nobody is above or below us.

You can build such qualities that are keys to success.

If one client is taking all your time, reassess his or her value.

If the contract is no longer rewarding, end it as soon as possible.

Doesn't matter if it is a business or personal relationship.

You must get clear on the fact that you are working for you.

You should consider no one your boss.

You should view whoever pays you as a client,

As such you should provide them the best service you can.

Always look to create more opportunity for your business.

Don't look for security - it doesn't exist.

Even if you find it for a time, I guarantee it will be boring at best.

Look for productivity and progression.

Change is definite. It is the only constant.

It will be up to you whether it is progression or regression.

Work with people who have similar goals and objectives.

You should always work with, never for.

Remember that you are always working for yourself.

If working with a company is not bringing you any closer to your goal,

End it now and find one that will.

You should never feel stuck in a job because leaving it is only a letter or phone call away.

You can replace that income in a million different ways.

If you don't like someone scheduling your week for you, start your own business.

If you don't know how, get the training.

Investing in your skills is an investment in your future.

Learning doesn't end with high school.

That was only the beginning – that was practice

Be a life-long learner.

Learn on the job.

Learn so you can achieve more.

Once you admit that you are working for you,

change your bosses title to 'client'.

Open your eyes to a world of other big and wonderful opportunities.

Realize that you are more valuable than you previously believed yourself to be.

Believe you will are incredibly valuable, and you deserve to be paid accordingly.

Whether you are a minimum wage worker or a company director,

you probably haven't even scratched the surface of your capabilities.

Every time someone places limits on what is possible, somebody proves them wrong.

You work for yourself, the possibilities are limitless.

Chapter 7:

How To Succeed In Life

"You can't climb the ladder of success with your hands in your pocket."

Every day that you're living, make a habit of making the most out of it. Make a habit of winning today. Don't dwell on the past, don't worry about the future. You just have to make sure that you're winning today. Move a little forward every day; take a little step every day. And when you're giving your fruitful efforts, you're making sure you're achieving your day, then you start to built confidence within yourselves. Confidence is when you close your eyes at night and see a vision, a dream, a goal, and you believe that you're going to achieve it. When you're doing things, when you're productive the whole day, then that long journey will become short in a matter of time.

Make yourself a power list for each day. Take a sheet of paper, write Monday on top of it and then write five critical, productive, actionable tasks that you're going to do that day. After doing the task, cross it off. Repeat the process every day of every week of every month till you get closer to achieving your goals, your dreams. It doesn't matter if you're doing the same tasks every day or how minor or major they are; what matters is that it's creating momentum in things that you've believed you couldn't do. And as soon as the momentum gets completed, you start to believe that you can do something. You eventually stop writing your tasks down because now they've become your new habits. You need a reminder for them. You don't need to cross them off because you're going to do them. The power list helps you win the day. You're stepping out of your comfort zone, doing something that looks uncomfortable for starters, but while doing this, even for a year, you will see yourself standing five years from where you're standing today.

Decide, commit, act, succeed, repeat. If you want to be an inspiration to others, a motivator to others, impact others somehow, you have to self-evaluate certain perceptions and think that'll help you change the way you see yourself and the world. Perseverance, hard-working, and consistency would be the keywords if one were to achieve success in life. You just have to keep yourself focused on your ultimate goal. You will fall a hundred times. There's always stumbling on the way. But if you have the skill, the power, the instinct to get yourself back up every time you fall, and to dig yourself out of the whole, then no one can stop you. You have to control the situation, Don't ever let the situation control you. You're living life exactly as it should be. If you don't like what you're living in, then consider changing the aspects. The person you are right now versus the person you want to be in the future, there's only a fine line between the two that you have to come face-to-face with.

Your creativity is at most powerful the moment you open your eyes and start your day. That's when you get the opportunity to steer your emotions and thoughts in the direction that you want them to go, not the other way around. Every failure is a step closer to success. We won't succeed on the first try, and we will never have it perfect by trying it only once. But we can master the art of not giving up. We dare to take risks. If we never fail, we never get the chance of getting something we never had. We can never taste the fruits of success without falling. The difference between successful people and those who aren't successful is the point of giving up.

Success isn't about perfection. Instead, it's about getting out of bed each day, clearing the dust off you, and thinking like a champion, a winner, going on about your day, being productive, and making the most out of it. Remember that the mind controls your body; your body doesn't hold your mind. You have to make yourself mentally tough to overcome the fears and challenges that come in the way of your goals. As soon as you get up in the morning, start thinking about anything or anyone that you're grateful for. Your focus should be on making yourself feel good and confident enough to get yourself through the day.

The negative emotions that we experience, like pain or rejection, or frustration, cannot always make our lives miserable. Instead, we can consider them as our most incredible friends that'll drive us to success. When people succeed, they tend to party. When they fail, they tend to ponder. And the pondering helps us get the most victories in our lives. You're here, into another day, still breathing fine, that means you got another chance, to better yourself, to be able to right your wrongs. Everyone has a more significant potential than the roles they put themselves in.

Trust yourself always. Trust your instinct—no matter what or how anyone thinks. You're perfectly capable of doing things your way. Even if they go wrong, you always learn something from them. Don't ever listen to the naysayers. You've probably heard a million times that you can't do this and you can't do that, or it's never even been done before. So what? So what if no one has ever done it before. That's more of the reason for you to do it since you'll become the first person to do it. Change that 'You can't' into 'Yes, I definitely can.' Muhammad Ali, one of the greatest boxers to walk on the face of this planet, was once asked, 'how many sit-ups do you do?' to which he replied, 'I don't count my sit-ups. I only start counting when it starts hurting. When I feel pain, that's when I start counting because that's when it really counts.' So we get a wonderful lesson to work tirelessly and shamelessly if we were to achieve our dreams. Dr. Arnold Schwarzenegger beautifully summed up life's successes in 6 simple rules; Trust yourself, Break some rules, Don't be afraid to fail, Ignore the naysayers, Work like hell, And give something back.

Chapter 8:

How to Learn Faster

Remember the saying, "You are never too old to learn something new"? Believe me, it's not true in any way you understood it.

The most reliable time to learn something new was the time when you were growing up. That was the time when your brain was in its most hyperactive state and could absorb anything you had thrown at it.

You can still learn, but you would have to change your approach to learning.

You won't learn everything, because you don't like everything going on around you. You naturally have an ego to please. So what can you do to boost your learning? Let's simplify the process. When you decide to learn something, take a moment and ask yourself this; "Will this thing make my life better? Will this fulfill my dreams? Will I benefit from it?".

If you can answer all these questions in a positive, you will pounce on the thing and you won't find anyone more motivated than you.

Learning is your brain's capability to process things constructively. If you pick up a career, you won't find it hard to flourish if you are genuinely interested in that particular skill.

Whether it be sports, singing, entrepreneurship, cooking, writing, or anything you want to pursue. Just ask yourself, can you use it to increase your creativity, your passion, your satisfaction. If you can, you will start learning it as if you knew it all along.

Your next step to learning faster would be to improve and excel at what you already have. How can you do that? It's simple yet again!

Ask yourself another question, that; "Why must I do this? Why do I need this?" if you get to answer that, you will find the fastest and effective way to the top yourself without any coaching. Why will this happen on its own? Because now you have found a purpose for your craft and the destination is clear as the bright sun in the sky.

The last but the most important thing to have a head start on your journey of learning is the simplest of them all, but the hardest to opt for. The most important step is to start working towards things.

The flow of learning is from Head to Heart to Hands. You have thought of the things you want to do in your brain. Then you asked your heart if it satisfied you. Now it's time to put your hands to work.

You never learn until you get the chance to experience the world yourself. When you go through a certain event, your brain starts to process the outcomes that could have been, and your heart tells you to give it one more try. Here is the deciding moment. If you listen to your heart right away, you will get on a path of learning that you have never seen before.

What remains now is your will to do what you have decided. And when you get going, you will find the most useful resources immediately. Use your instincts and capitalize your time. Capture every chance with sheer will and belief as if this is your final moment for your dreams to come true.

It doesn't matter if you are not the ace in the pack, it doesn't matter if you are not in your peak physical shape, it doesn't matter if you don't have the money yet. You will someday get all those things only if you had the right skills and the right moment.

For all you know, this moment right now is the most worth it moment. So don't go fishing in other tanks when you have your own aquarium. That aquarium is your body, mind, and soul. All you need is to dive deep with sheer determination and the stars are your limit.

=

Chapter 9:
The Things That Matter

Today we're going to talk about a topic that I am very passionate about. Passionate because it has helped to guide each and every decision that I make on a daily basis. Having this constant reminder of the things that matter will put things in perspective for us - to eliminate the things that are taking up our time for the wrong reasons and to focus on the things that we actually want deep down in our hearts.

With that in mind, let's begin.

How many of you can safely say that you know what truly matters in life? How do you define living a successful and fulfilling life? Is it by having a certain net worth? Is it by living a stress-free life? Is it seeing the world? Is it by serving a defined number of people? Is it by having 10 life-long friends that you can count on? Is it by having a certain number of kids? Or have you not really thought about what you really want out of life yet?

Before we can really gear our actions towards the direction that we want to lead it, we must first know exactly what those specific things we want to achieve are.

The things that matter in my life vary over time as I get older and wiser. When I was young I used to think getting good grades, getting into a good university, and getting a good and stable job was all that really mattered, but I have soon come to realize that family, friends, and having people to hang out with were way more important than simply making money. There was a point in my life that I was so driven by money that I created a huge imbalance in my life by spending 99% of my time on my career. This lopsided drive caused me to neglect friendships, relationships, and soon people associated me with always being too busy for anything. I gradually stopped hanging out with anyone altogether. At first it was okay as I thought "hey, I finally have time to do whatever I want" and I don't have to be disturbed by meetups that would disrupt my workflow. But over time, I felt a gaping hole opening up somewhere deep inside that I could not seem to fill. I suddenly realized that I had successfully isolated myself from any and all relationships. This isolation felt increasingly lonely for me. I felt that I had no one to talk to when I was feeling down, no one to share my struggles with, no one to walk this journey with, and I knew I needed to do something about it. It was only after I started reconnecting with my friends did I truly feel alive again. Having friends brought me more joy than money ever did or could. There's a saying that you can't buy happiness; the same is true for friendships - you can't buy them either. They have to be earned and built with trust and loyalty.

For those of you who are so career focused and money-minded, I share from experience that the destination may not be pretty if you do not have friends or family to share it with. Sure you may afford a penthouse or a Ferrari, but what does it really mean? Sure you have a nice view and a fast ride, but can you share your life with it? When you are old and frail, can your house and car support you physically and emotionally? Don't make the same mistake I did for a good 3 years of my life. It was enough time for me to feel completely alone. No amount of acquiring things could fill that hole no matter how hard I tried. Sure I had the fanciest Apple products, my iPad, iPhone, MacBook, iMac, AirPods, the list goes on. Sure I could "make friends" with these shiny objects by using them everyday. But over time it just reminded me more and more that I had replaced people with gadgets, that I had replaced humans with Siri. It was really really sad honestly.

Having friends that don't judge you or who don't care whether you have money or not, those are the real friends that you know you can count on. And I urge those of you who have neglected this big part to start reconnecting old friends or finding new ones altogether who share the same interests as you. Golf buddies, tennis buddies, karaoke buddies, these are good places to start searching for friends and getting the ice broken.

If starting a family is something that you really want in life, have you begun searching for a partner and planning how and when you expect that to happen for you? Sure many of us think we may have a lot of time to do after we get our career going, but how many of us have heard stories of people who just never got off the bandwagon because they've become too busy with their careers? That maybe getting pregnant just never seems like the right time because you don't want to jeopardize your job. Or maybe that you never even got around to dating at all by the time you are 35 because you've become too busy being a general manager of your company. If having a career is the most important thing to you, then by all means go full steam ahead to achieve that goal. However if family is something of great significance to you, you may want to consider starting that timeline right now instead of waiting. Remember the goal is to focus on the things that truly matter. If having a loving spouse who you can grow old with and having say 2 kids who can support you when you are old is what you really want, maybe waiting isn't such a good idea. Finding love takes practice. You will meet frogs along the way and it takes time to grow a lasting relationship. Sure you can rush a marriage if time is of the essence, but is that ideal? Personally I believe a strong relationship takes 2-3 years to build. Do you have that type of runway to play with? Don't work yourself to death at your job only to find yourself rich and alone. Regret will come after for sure.

Whatever else you have defined as the things that matter to you, make sure that you never neglect those priorities. Sometimes life gets so busy and hectic that we forget to stop and refresh ourselves on what we really want to get out of life. It is all too easy for us to operate on autopilot - To set an alarm, go to work, gym, go home, take dinner, sleep, and repeat the day all over again. For weekends, we may be so exhausted from work that we just end up sleeping or wasting our weekend away only to begin the same routine again on Monday.

There's plenty of time for work decades down the road, but dating relationships and friendships may not have that runway of time.

So I challenge each and everyone of you to clearly define what the things that matter mean to you and to take consistent action in these areas day in and out until you can safely say you've already checked them off your bucket list. Take care and I'll see you in the next one.

Chapter 10:

First Impressions Matter

Today we're going to talk about a simple topic that I hope will help each and every one of you make a good first impression in every meeting you may encounter in the future.

So why bother with making a good first impression in the first place? The answer is fairly simple - people decide very quickly in the first few minutes whether they think you are someone they might want to associate themselves with or not. They see how you look, how you dress, how you carry yourself, and they decide usually fairly quickly about what label they want to tag on you. Humans are judgemental and superficial creatures by nature. Barring all other aspects of your personality, how you look is the first thing that others can deduce about you.

We have all done this at some point in our lives - we make sweeping remarks about the first "hot guy" or "hot girl" that we see, and we we remark at the way they dress and the choices that they make stylistically. We may find ourself immediately attracted to them based on just their looks.

Of course how we carry ourselves is equally important as well. When we go for interviews, when we meet new clients, the vibes that we let out matters. How others perceive us in that first meeting will set the tone on whether we may be asked back for a second interview, or if our clients will continue to decide on whether to work with us moving forward. Sure if we don't do well in the first impression we may have a chance to redeem ourselves in the second chance we get, but I'm sure that's not where you want to end up if given the choice.

So how can we do our best to make a good first impression in any situation?

I want to start by making sure that you know who your audience is. Do your homework and try your best to anticipate what the opposing party might aspect of you. If you are going for a job interview and you know it will be a formal one, do your best to look smart and dress accordingly. Don't show up with your shirts untucked and un-ironed. Ensure that you look the part of the job you are gunning for. Sure things may go wrong during the interview, but at least you showed up looking like you really are serious about the job and that you want to look presentable for your future boss.

If you know that you are going on a first date for example, make a good first impression by also grooming yourself accordingly to attract your partner. I know it may sound incredibly superficial, but if you look into nature, almost all creatures have a way of attracting their mates. Whether it be through colourful feathers in a peacock, or dance rituals in some exotic birds, or a flowing mane of a lion, all these are ways to catch the attention of their potential partners. When someone dresses nicely it shows that they are making an effort to look good and that they are in the business of winning you over.

Now that I've given you some examples of how looking the part can give you a huge boost in your first impressions rating, I want to move on to the next part which is how you actually carry yourself through the things that you say and the actions that you take.

Everyone knows that a pretty face can only carry you so far if you don't have a good personality to match. Sure we may lust for something that looks good on the outside, but if we take a bite from it and it tastes absolutely gastly, I'm sure most of us would eventually run for the hills afterward. The same goes when you go for interviews as well.

The simplest advice I can give for all of you is to be yourself. Don't try to be something that you are not. In most situations, I believe that staying true to who you are and being congruent in what you say is very important. Yes you have to be professional and do your best to showcase your talents in your area of expertise, but beyond that we do need to try our best to be as authentic as possible. Depending on what our motives are and what we want to get out of the first impression meeting, we have to be really clear about our intentions. If our goal is to deceive, you may find it easy to lie our way through the first meeting, but the truth eventually catches up with us when the opposite party finds that we are not up for job or up to the standards that we have set for ourselves in the first session. If we had stayed true to ourselves from the very beginning, our words will hold more credit and questions to our integrity will be kept to a minimal.

If we want to attract a spouse that is kind-hearted and good-willed, it is only natural for us to expect the same if the opposing party gave us the impression that they are. If it was done out of deceit, over time it will slowly creep up as their authenticity stays to crack and we are revealed their true nature. If we expect others to act and behave the way that is congruent with what they show us in the first impression, we should also do the same for others.

Yes I know that I may be going off a tangent of creating good first impressions. But I am also not going to advocate here that we change ourself completely to make a good impression the first time around only to show up like totally different versions of ourselves the next. I always believe that staying true to who you are is the best way to not only make a good first impression, but also to make a lasting and permanent impression. We want to build a strong reputation for ourselves as individuals who are confident and competent at the same time. We want to earn others' trust not out of deceit but out of skill.

If we find ourselves lacking in certain areas, I propose that we work on it on a consistent and daily basis. If we find that maybe we're not happy with the way we look, make a commitment to get to the gym 5 times a week and to eat healthier. If we find ourselves lacking in key soft skills, we may want to take up a course or go for trainings that help us be better in these areas. If we find ourselves lacking in certain skill sets required for particular job that we want, we may want to consider getting further education so that we are qualified in those areas. The bottom line is, we should never stop working on ourselves. Only then can we truly make a powerful first impression that is credible and lasting.

So I challenge each and everyone of you today to make it a point to put making a good genuine first impression at the top of our list for every new person that we meet. Whatever the reason may be, dress up accordingly and present ourselves well so that we may hopefully get the thing that we want.

I hope you learned something today. Take care and I'll see you in the next one.

PART 3

Chapter 1:

Doing The Thing You Love Most

Today we are going to talk about following your heart and just going for your passion, even if it ends up being a hobby project.

Many of us have passions that we want to pursue. Whether it be a sport, a fitness goal, a career goal, or simply just doing something we know we are good at. Something that electrifies our soul. Something that really doesn't require much persuasion for us to just go do it on a whim.

Many of us dare not pursue this passion because people have told us time and time again that it will not lead to anywhere. Or maybe it is that voice inside your head that is telling you you should just stick to the practical things in life. Whatever the reasons may be, that itch always seem to pester us, calling out to us, even though we have tried our best to put it aside.

We know what our talents are, and the longer we don't put it out there in the world, the longer we keep it bottled up inside of us, the longer the we will regret it. Personally, Music has always been something that has been calling out to me since i was 15. I've always dabbled in and out of it, but never took it seriously. I found myself 14 years later, wondering how much i could've achieved in the music space if i had just leaned in to it just a little.

I decided that I had just about put it off for long enough and decided to pursue music part time. I just knew deep down inside me that if i did not at least try, that i was going to regret it at some point again in the future. It is true that passions come and go. We may jump from passion to passion over the course of our lives, and that is okay. But if that thing has been there calling out to you for years or even decades, maybe you should pay closer attention to it just a little more.

Make your passion a project. Make it a hobby. Pursue it in one form or another. We may never be able to make full careers out of our passions, but we can at least incorporate it into our daily lives like a habit. You may find ourselves happier and more fulfilled should you tap that creative space in you that has always been there.

Sure life still takes precedence. Feeding the family, earning that income, taking care of that child. But never for one second think that you should sacrifice doing what truly makes you happy for all of that other stuff, no matter how important. Even as a hobby, pursuing it maybe 30mins a day, or even just an hour a week. It is a start and it is definitely better than nothing.

At the end of the day passions are there to feed our soul. To provide it will some zest and life to our otherwise mundane lives. The next time you hear that voice again, lean in to it. Don't put it off any longer.

Chapter 2:

Dealing With Difficult People

It is inevitable that people will rub us the wrong way as we go about our days. Dealing with such people requires a lot of patience and self-control, especially if they are persistent in their actions towards you over a lengthy period of time.

Difficult people are outside the realm of our control and hence we need to implement strategies to deal with negative emotions should they arise. If you encounter such people frequently, here are 7 ways that you can take back control of the situation.

1.   Write Your Feelings Down Immediately

A lot of times we bottle up feelings when someone is rude or unpleasant to us. We may have an urge to respond but in the moment we choose not to. In those circumstances, the next best thing we can do is to write down our feelings either in our journals or in our smartphones as notes.

Writing our feelings down is a therapeutic way to cleanse our thoughts and negative energy. In writing we can say the things we wished we had said, and find out the reasons that made us feel uneasy in the first place. In writing we are also able to clearly identify the trigger points and could work backwards in managing our expectations and feelings around the person. If it is a rude customer, or a rude stranger, we may not be able to respond for fear or retaliation or for fear of losing our jobs. It is best those situations not to erupt in anger, but take the time to work through those emotions in writing.

2.   Tell The Person Directly What You Dislike About Their Attitude

If customer service and retail isn't your profession, or if it is not your boss, you may have the power to voice your opinion directly to the person who wronged you. If confrontation is something that you are comfortable with, don't hesitate to express to them why you are dissatisfied with their treatment or attitude towards you. You may also prefer to clear your head before coming back to confront the person and not let emotions escalate. A fight is the last thing we want out of this communication.

3. Give An Honest Feedback Where Possible On Their Website

If physical confrontation is not your cup of tea, consider writing in a feedback online to express your dissatisfaction. We are usually able to write the most clear and precise account of the situation when we have time to process what went wrong. Instead of handling this confrontation ourselves, the Human Resources team would most likely deal with this person directly, saving you the trouble in the process. Make sure to give an accurate account of the situation and not exaggerate the contents to make the person look extremely in the wrong, although it can be tough to contain our emotions when we are so riled up.

4. Use this Energy To Fuel Your Fire

Sometimes, taking all these energy and intense emotions we feel may fuel our fire to work harder or to prove to others that we are not deserving of their hatred. Be careful though not to take things too far. Remember that ultimately you have the power to choose whether to let this person affect you. If you choose to accept these emotions, use them wisely.

5. Channel This Intense Emotion Into A Craft That Allows You To Release Unwanted Feelings

For those who have musical talents, we may use this negative experience to write a song about it while we are at the heights of our emotions. In those moments the feelings are usually intense, and we all know that emotions can sometimes produce the best works of art. If playing an instrument, writing an article, producing a movie clip, or crushing a sport is something that comes natural to us, we may channel and convert these emotions into masterpieces. Think Adele, Taylor Swift, and all the great songwriters of our generation as an example.

6.   Learn To Grow Your Patience

Sometimes not saying anything at all could be the best course of action. Depending on the type of person you are, and the level of zen you have in you, you may not be so easily phased by negativity if you have very high control of your emotions. Through regular meditation and deep breathing, we can let go of these bad vibes that people send our way and just watch it vanish into a cloud of smoke. Regular yoga and meditation practices are good ways to train and grow your patience.

7.   Stand Up For Yourself

At the end of the day, you have to choose when and if you want to stand up for yourself if someone has truly wronged you. We can only be so patient and kind to someone before we snap. Never be afraid to speak your truth and defend yourself if you feel that you have been wrongfully judged. Difficult people make our lives unpleasant but it doesn't mean we should allow them to walk all over us without consequences. You have every right to fight for your rights, even if it means giving up something important in the process to defend it.

Chapter 3:

Dealing With Addiction To Technology

Today we're going to talk about addiction to technology and media consumption. I think this is a topic that many of us can relate, even myself included. Am my goal for today is to try to help put forth a more sustainable and healthy habit for you to still enjoy technology while not being overwhelmed and overtaken by it completely.

So lets ask ourselves a simple question of why are we so hooked into using our devices so frequently and sparingly? I think for most of us, and this is my personal opinion, is that it offers us an escape, a distraction from our every day tasks that we know we ought to do. To procrastinate just a little bit or to binge scroll on Instagram, Facebook, Snapchat, and what have you, to satisfy our need for media consumption.

We use technology as a tool a gateway into the world of digital media, and we get lost in it because companies try to feed us with posts and stuff that we like to keep us engaged and to keep us watching just a little while longer. And minutes can turn into hours, and before you know it, it is bedtime.

I want to argue that this addiction is not entirely your fault, but that these multi billion dollar mega companies are being fed so much data that they are able to manipulate us into consume their media. It is like how casinos use various tricks of flickering lights, and free drinks to keep you playing a little longer and to spend a little more of your attention and time. We unknowingly get subjected to these manipulative tactics and we fall for it despite our best efforts to abstain from it.

I for one have been the subject of such manipulation. Whether it be Netflix or my favourite social media apps, I find myself mindlessly scrolling through posts trying to get my quick fix of distraction and supposed stress relief. However these feelings dont bring me joy, rather it brings me anxiety that I have wasted precious time and I end up kicking myself for it afterwards. This happens time and time again and it felt like I was stuck in a loop, unable to get out.

So what is the solution to this seemingly endless spiral of bad habits? Some might say just to delete the apps, or turn off wifi. But how many of you might have actually tried that yourself only to have it backfire on you? Redownloading the app is only one step away, wifi is only one button away, and addictions aren't so easily kicked to the curb as one might think.

What I have found that works is that instead of consuming mindless media that don't bring about actual benefit to my life, I chose to watch content that I could actually learn something from. Like this channel for example. I went on the hunt to seek out content that I could learn how to make extra money, how to improve my health, how to improve my relationships, basically anything that had to do with personal development. And I found that I actually felt less guilty watching or reading these posts even though they still do take up my time to consume.

You may call it a lesser of two evils, but what I discovered was that it provided much more benefit to my life than actually not consuming any personal development media at all. Whether it be inspirational stories from successful entrepreneurs like Elon Musk, or Jeff Bezos, or multi billion dollar investment advice from Warren Buffet, these passive watching of useful content actually boosted my knowledge in areas that I might otherwise have not been exposed to. Subconsciously, i started internalizing some of these beliefs and adopted it into my own psyche. And i transformed what was mindless binge watching of useless Tv shows and zombie content, to something that actually moved the needle in my life in the right direction, even by a little.

Overtime, I actually required less and less distraction of media consumption using my technology devices like iPhones and iPads or Macs, and started putting more attention and effort to do the work that I knew i had to get done. Because some of these personal development videos actually taught me what I needed to do to get stuff done and to stop procrastinating in working towards my goals.

So I challenge each and everyone of you today to do a thorough review of the kinds of music and media consumption that you consume today with your smartphones and tablets, and see if you can substitute them with something that you can learn from, no matter how trivial you think it may be. It could be the very push you need to start porting over all your bad habits of technology into something that can pay off for you 10 years down the road.

I hope you learned something today, and I'll see you in the next one.

Chapter 4:

Block Out The Critics and Detractors

There is drama everywhere around us. In fact, our whole life is a drama. A drama that has more complex turns and thrillers than the best thriller ever to be made on a cinema screen.

This drama isn't always a result of our own actions. Sometimes we do something stupid to contribute towards anarchy. But mostly the things happening around us seem to be a drama because the critics make a hell out of everything.

We get sucked into things that and someone else's opinions because we do not know what we are doing.

It may sound cliche but remember that it doesn't matter what anyone else says. In fact, most discoveries and inventions got bad press when they were found or made. It was only after they are gone when people actually came to appreciate the true importance of those inventions.

The time will come sooner or later when you are finally appreciated for your work and your effort. But your work should not depend on what others will say.

Your work should not depend on the hope of appreciation or the fear of criticism, rather it should be done because it was meant to be done. You should put your heart and soul in it because you had a reason for all this and only you will reap the fruit, no matter what the world gets from it.

You don't need to do the best out there in the world and neither should you be judged on that standard. But you should put out the best YOU can do because that will someday shut out the critics as they start to see your true potential.

The work itself doesn't matter, but the effort you put behind it does. You don't need to be an insult to anyone who mocks you or criticizes you on even your best work. Empathy is your best approach to bullying.

You cannot possibly shut out every critic. You spend your whole life trying to answer to those meaningless least important people that weren't even able to make their own lives better. Because those who did make something of themselves didn't find it worthwhile to distract and degrade everyone else.

So you should try to spend your time more and more on your good work. Keep a straight sight without even thinking to look at one more ordinary critic who doesn't give a simple feeling of empathy towards your efforts.

You only need to put yourself in others' shoes and look at yourself through their eyes. If you can do that before them, you would have the best reply to any hurtful comment. And that my friend will be true silence.

People always come to gather around you when they see a cause they can relate to. So give them a cause. Give a ray of hope and motivation to people around you and you will finally get to get the critics on your side.

Your critics will help you get to the top from the hardest side there is.

Chapter 5:

Distraction Is Robbing You

Every second you spend doing something that is not moving you
towards your goal, you are robbing yourself of precious time.
Stop being distracted!

You have something you need to do,
but for some reason become distracted by
other less important tasks and procrastinate on the important stuff.
Most people do it,
whether it's notification s on your phone or chat with colleges,
mostly less than half the working day is productive.

Distraction can be avoided by having a schedule
which should include some down time to relax
or perhaps get some of them distractions out of the way,
but time limited.

As long as everything has its correct time in
your day you can keep distraction from stealing too much of your time.
When your mind is distracted it becomes nearly impossible to
concentrate on the necessary work at hand.
Always keep this question in mind:
"is what I am about to do moving me towards my goal?"

If not, is it necessary?

What could I do instead that will?

It's all about your 24 hours.

Your actions and the reactions to your actions from that day,

good or bad.

By keeping your mind focused on your schedule that

moves you towards your goal, you will become resilient to distraction.

Distraction is anything that is not on your schedule.

You may need to alter that depending on the importance of the

intrusion.

Being successful means becoming single minded about your goal.

Those with faith do not need a plan b because they know plan A is the

only way and they refuse to accept anything else.

Any time you spend contemplating failure will add to its chances of

happening.

Why not focus on what will happen if you succeed instead?

Distraction from your vision of success is one of its biggest threats.

Blocking out distraction and keeping that vision clear is key.

Put that phone on flight mode and turn off the TV.

Focus on the truly important stuff.

If you don't do it, it will never get done.

The responsibility is all yours for everything in your life.

The responsibility is yours to block out the distractions and exercise your free-will over your thoughts and actions.

By taking responsibility and control you will become empowered.
Refuse to let anyone distract you when you're working.
Have a set time in your schedule to deal with stuff not on the schedule.
This will allow you time to deal with unexpected issues without stopping you doing the original work.
The reality is that we all only have so much time.
Do you really want to waste yours on distractions?
Do you want to not hit your target because of them?
Every time you stop for a notification on your phone you are losing time from your success.
Don't let distraction rob you of another second, minute, hour or day.
Days turn to months and months turn to years don't waste time on distractions and fears.

Chapter 6:

Discovering Your Purpose

If you guys don't already know, this is one of the topics that I really love talking about. And I never get tired of it. Having a purpose is something that I always believe everyone should have. Having a purpose to live, to breathe, to get up each day, I believe that without purpose, there is no point to life.

So today we're going to talk about how to discover your purpose, and why you should make it a point to find one if you didn't already start looking.

So what is purpose exactly. A purpose is a reason to do something. Is to have something else greater than ourselves to work for. You see, I believe if we are only focused on ourselves, instead of others, we will not be able to be truly happy in life. Feeding our own self interests does not bring us joy as one might think. After living the life that I had, I realized that true happiness only comes when you bring joy to someone else's life. Whether it be helping others professionally or out of selflessness, this happiness will radiate and reflect back to us from someone else who is appreciative of your efforts.

On some level, we can look into ourselves to be happy. For example being grateful for life, loving ourselves, and all that good stuff. Yes keep doing those things. But there is a whole other dimension if we devote our time and energy into helping others once we have already conquered ourselves. If you look at many of the most successful people on the planet, after they have acquired an immense amount of wealth, many of them look to passion projects or even philanthropy where they can give back to the community when having more money doesn't do anything for them anymore. If you look at Elon Musk and Jeff Bezos, these two have a greater purpose which is their space projects. Where they visualise humans being able to move out of Earth one day where civilisation is able to expand. Or Bill Gates and Warren Buffet, who have pledged to give billions of their money away for philanthropic work, to help the less fortunate and to fund organisations that work towards finding cures to diseases.

Now for us mere mortals, we don't need to think so big. Our purpose need not be so extravagant. It can be as simple as having a purpose to provide for your loved one, to work hard to bring your family members of holidays and travel, or to bring joy to your elderly relatives by organising activities for them to do. There is no purpose that is too big or too small.

Your purpose could be helping others find a beautiful home, doing charitable work, or even feeding and providing for your growing family.

As humans, we will automatically work harder if we have a clear and defined purpose. We have a reason to get up each day, to go to work, to earn that paycheck, so that we can spend it on things and people, even ourselves at times. Without a purpose, we struggle to find meaning in the work that we do. We struggle to see the big picture and we find that we have no reason to work so hard, or even at all. And we struggle to find life worth living.

This revelation came to me when I started seeing my work as helping some other person in a meaningful way. Where my work was not just about making money to buy nice things, but to be able to impact someone else's life in a positive way. That became my purpose. To see them learn something new, and to bring a joy and smile to their faces. That thought that I was contributing something useful to someone made me smile more than money ever could. Yes money can help you live a comfortable life, but helping others can go a much farther way into giving your life true purpose.

So I challenge each and everyone of you to find a purpose in everything that you do, and if you struggle to find one, start by making the goal to help others a priority. Think of the difference you can make to others and that could very well be your purpose in life as well.

I believe in each and every one of you.. I hope you learned something today and as always, take care and I'll see you in the next one.

Discomfort Is Temporary

It's easy to get hopeless when things get a little overwhelming. It's easy to give up because you feel you don't have the strength or resources to continue. But where you stop is actually the start you have been looking for since the beginning.

Do you know what you should do when you are broken? You should relish it. You should use it. Because if you know you are broken, congratulations, you have found your limitations.

Now as you know what stopped you last time, you can work towards mending it. You can start to reinforce the breach and you should be able to fill in the cracks in no time.

Life never repeats everything. One day you feel the lowest and the next might bring you the most unpredictable gifts.

The world isn't all sunshine and rainbows. It is a very mean and nasty place to be in. But what can you do now when you are in it? Nothing? Never!

You have to endure the pain, the stress, the discomfort till you are comfortable with the discomfort. It doesn't make any sense, right? But listen to me.

You have a duty towards yourself. You have a duty towards your loved ones. You are expected to rise above all odds and be something no one has ever been before you. I know it might be a little too much to ask for, but, you have to understand your purpose.

Your purpose isn't just to sit on your back and the opportunities and blessings keep coming, knocking at your door, just so you can give up one more time and turn them down.

Things are too easy to reject and neglect but always get hard when you finally step up and go for them. But remember, every breathtaking view is from the top of a hill, but the trek to the top is always tiring. But when you get to the top, you find every cramp worth it.

If you are willing to put yourself through anything, discomfort and temporary small intervals of pain won't affect you in any way. As long as you believe that the experience will bring you to a new level.

If you are interested in the unknown, then you have to break barriers and cross your limits. Because every path that leads to success is full of them. But then and only then you will find yourself in a place where you are unbreakable.

You need to realize that your life is better than most people out there. You need to embrace the pain because all this is temporary. But when you are finally ready to embrace the pain, you are already on your way to a superior being.

Life is all about taking stands because we all get all kinds of blows. But we always need to dig in and keep fighting till we have found the gems or have found our last breath.

The pain and discomfort will subside one day, but if you quit, then you are already on the end of your rope.

Chapter 7:

Discomfort Is Temporary

It's easy to get hopeless when things get a little overwhelming. It's easy to give up because you feel you don't have the strength or resources to continue. But where you stop is actually the start you have been looking for since the beginning.

Do you know what you should do when you are broken? You should relish it. You should use it. Because if you know you are broken, congratulations, you have found your limitations.

Now as you know what stopped you last time, you can work towards mending it. You can start to reinforce the breach and you should be able to fill in the cracks in no time.

Life never repeats everything. One day you feel the lowest and the next might bring you the most unpredictable gifts.

The world isn't all sunshine and rainbows. It is a very mean and nasty place to be in. But what can you do now when you are in it? Nothing? Never!

You have to endure the pain, the stress, the discomfort till you are comfortable with the discomfort. It doesn't make any sense, right? But listen to me.

You have a duty towards yourself. You have a duty towards your loved ones. You are expected to rise above all odds and be something no one has ever been before you. I know it might be a little too much to ask for, but, you have to understand your purpose.

Your purpose isn't just to sit on your back and the opportunities and blessings keep coming, knocking at your door, just so you can give up one more time and turn them down.

Things are too easy to reject and neglect but always get hard when you finally step up and go for them. But remember, every breathtaking view is from the top of a hill, but the trek to the top is always tiring. But when you get to the top, you find every cramp worth it.

If you are willing to put yourself through anything, discomfort and temporary small intervals of pain won't affect you in any way. As long as you believe that the experience will bring you to a new level.

If you are interested in the unknown, then you have to break barriers and cross your limits. Because every path that leads to success is full of them. But then and only then you will find yourself in a place where you are unbreakable.

You need to realize that your life is better than most people out there. You need to embrace the pain because all this is temporary. But when you are finally ready to embrace the pain, you are already on your way to a superior being.

Life is all about taking stands because we all get all kinds of blows. But we always need to dig in and keep fighting till we have found the gems or have found our last breath.

The pain and discomfort will subside one day, but if you quit, then you are already on the end of your rope.

Chapter 8:

Being Mentally Strong

Have you ever wondered why your performance in practice versus an actual test is like night and day? Or how you are able to perform so well in a mock situation but just crumble when it comes game time?

It all boils down to our mental strength.

The greatest players in sports all have one thing in common, incredibly strong beliefs in themselves that they can win no matter how difficult the circumstance. Where rivals that have the same playing ability may challenge them, they will always prevail because they know their self-worth and they never once doubt that they will lose even when facing immense external or internal pressure.

Most of us are used to facing pressure from external sources. Whether it be from people around us, online haters, or whoever they may be, that can take a toll on our ability to perform. But the greatest threat is not from those areas... it is from within. The voices in our head telling us that we are not going to win this match, that we are not going to well in this performance, that we should just give up because we are already losing by that much.

It is only when we can crush these voices that we can truly outperform our wildest abilities. Mental strength is something that we can all acquire. We just have to find a way to block out all the negativity and replace them with voices that are encouraging. to believe in ourselves that we can and will overcome any situation that life throws at us.

The next time you notice that doubts start creeping in, you need to snap yourself out of it as quickly as you can, 5 4 3 2 1. Focus on the next point, focus on the next game, focus on the next speech. Don't give yourself the time to think about what went wrong the last time. You are only as good as your present performance, not your past.

I believe that you will achieve wonderful things in life you are able to crush those negative thoughts and enhance your mental strength.

Being Authentic

Today we're going to talk about the topic of authenticity. This topic is important because for many of us, we are told to put on a poker face and to act in ways that are politically correct. We are told by our parents, Teachers, and many other figures of authority to try to change who we are to fit society's norms and standards. Over time this constant act of being told to be different can end up forcing us to be someone who we are not entirely.

We start to behave in ways that are not true to ourselves. We start to act and say things that might start to appear rehearsed and fake, and we might not even notice this change until we hear whispers from colleagues or friends of friends that tell us we appear to be a little fake. On some level it isn't our fault as well, or it might be. Whatever the reason is, what we can do however is to make the effort to be more authentic.

So why do we need to be authentic? Well technically there's no one real reason that clearly defines why this is important. It actually depends on what we want to expect from others and in life in general. If we want to develop close bonds and friendships, it requires us to be honest and to be real. Our friends can tell very easily when it seems we are trying to hide something or if we are not being genuine or deceptive in the things we say. If people manage to detect that we are insincerity, they might easily choose to not be our friend or may start to distance themselves from us. If we are okay with that, then i guess being authentic is not a priority in this area.

When we choose to be authentic, we are telling the world that we are not afraid to speak our mind, that we are not afraid to be vocal of our opinions and not put on a mask to try and hide and filter how we present ourselves. Being authentic also helps people trust you more easily. When you are real with others, they tend to be real with you too. And this helps move the partnership along more quickly. Of course if this could also be a quick way to get into conflicts if one doesn't practice abit of caution in the things that they say that might be hurtful.

Being authentic builds your reputation as someone who is relatable. As humans we respond incredibly well to people who come across as genuine, kind, and always ready to help you in times of need. The more you open up to someone, they can connect with you on a much deeper emotional connection.

If you find yourself struggling with building lasting friendships, stop trying to be someone who you are not. You are not Kim Kardashian, Justin Bieber, or someone else. You are you, and you are beautiful. If there are areas of yourself you feel are lacking, work on it. But make sure you never try to hide the real you from others. You will find that life is much easier when you stop putting on a mask and just embracing and being you are meant to be all along.

I challenge each and everyone of you to consider adding authenticity into everything that you do. Let me know the changes that you have experienced as a result of that. I hope you learned something today, thank you so much for being there and I'll see you in the next one.

Chapter 9:

<u>Be Inspired to Create</u>

Some of you will look in the mirror today and think that you are weird. You will see that you are different to other people. That you are quirky or odd. But I want to encourage you. Not only is your uniqueness something that you should embrace but it is perhaps your greatest asset. The wonderful thing about people being different is that they think a little differently, see the world from a slightly different perspective. The combination of the various bits of knowledge that they have fit together in different ways.

When you speak you are most likely not conscious of your accent. Maybe if you live in a foreign country you are hyper aware of it. But how many of you know that your mind has an accent too. It has an accent that is formed from your experiences. Your experiences with pain. Your experiences with joy. Your experiences with success, failure and even your experiences with the everyday mundane. Not only that but the accent of your mind constantly evolves.

Why does that matter?

Because it is that accent which enables you to innovate. When you speak a foreign word, it takes on a new form in your accent – sometimes it may even be a sound that has never been uttered with that tone and inflection. It is completely original not because of the form of the word but because of the accent that informs the way the word comes out.

The same is true of your mind. You can speak the same ideas, study the same fields, even research the exact same thing and still end up with different outcomes. How? Because your outcomes are being informed by your experiences. Your ideas are your present thoughts running rampant through familiar thought patterns. They are tailored towards a particular style. For some of you it is like your mind rolls the r's in your ideas. It adds a certain *je ne sais quoi* to your ideas. To others your accent is thick and mutes the aesthetic nuances of ideas – manifesting in wonders of logic and mechanics.

Whatever it may be, I encourage you to embrace the accent of your mind. Actually, I demand you to. It is time that you stopped denying the world of your contribution to it. It's time that you got inspired to create. It is time that you allowed ideas to implode within the realm of your consciousness and innovations to pour out of it. Whether you find your language in art, dance, engineering, or politics. If you have a niche area of knowledge or see a pattern from a unique combination of information then it is about time you harnessed that and rode the creation train to wherever it may take you. I can promise you that you will never look back. We tend to regret the things we did not do, not the things that we did.

Listen closely and hear the accentuation of your thoughts. Then speak their creative ingenuity into being.

Create something that only you can.

Chapter 10:

Achieving Happiness

Happiness is a topic that is at the core of this channel. Because as humans we all want to be happy in some way shape or form. Happiness strikes as something that we all want to strive for because how can we imagine living an unhappy life. It might be possible but it wouldn't be all that fun no matter how you spin it. However I'm gonna offer another perspective that would challenge the notion of happiness and one that maybe would be more attainable for the vast majority of people.

So why do we as humans search for happiness? It is partly due to the fact that it has been ingrained in us since young that we all should strive to live a happy and healthy life. Happiness has become synonymous with the very nature of existence that when we find ourselves unhappy in any given moment, we tend to want to pivot our life and the current situation we are in to one that is more favourable, one that is supposedly able to bring us more happiness.

But how many of us are actually always happy all the time? I would argue that happiness is not at all sustainable if we were feeling it at full blast constantly. After a while we would find ourselves being numb to it and maybe that happiness would turn into neutrality or even boredom. There were times in my life where i felt truly happy and free. I felt that i had great friends around me, life had limitless possibilities, the weather was great, the housing situation was great, and i never wanted it to end as i knew that it was the best time of my life.

However knowing that this circumstance is only temporary allowed me to cherish each and every moment more meaningfully. As i was aware that time was not infinite and that some day this very state of happiness would somehow end one way or another, that i would use that time wisely and spend them with purpose and meaning. And it was this sense that nothing ever lasts forever that helped me gain a new perspective on everything i was doing at that present moment in time. Of course, those happy times were also filled with times of trials, conflicts, and challenges, and they made that period of my life all the more memorable and noteworthy.

For me, happiness is a temporary state that does not last forever. We might be happy today but sad tomorrow, but that is perfectly okay and totally fine. Being happy all the time is not realistic no matter how you spin it. The excitement of getting a new house and new car would soon fade from the moment you start driving in it, and that happiness you once thought you associated with it can disappear very quickly. And that is okay. Because life is about constant change and nothing really ever stays the same.

With happiness comes with it a whole host of different emotions that aims to highlight and enhance its feeling. Without sadness and sorrow, happiness would have no counter to be matched against. It is like a yin without a yang. And we need both in order to survive.

I believe that to be truly happy, one has to accept that sadness and feelings of unhappiness will come as a package deal. That whilst we want to be happy, we must also want to feel periods of lull to make the experience more rewarding.

I challenge all of you today to view happiness as not something that is static and that once you achieved it that all will be well and life will be good, but rather a temporary state of feeling that will come again and again when you take steps to seek it.

I also want to bring forth to you an alternative notion to happiness, in the form of contentment, that we will discuss in the next video. Take care and I'll see you there.

8 Things To Do When You Like Someone More Than You Thought You Would

Finding someone in life that can be your companion can be quite a journey. You will meet people who like to play games, who are wild and crazy, and those who are just downright unpleasant to be around. You will go on dates that you just want to quickly get out of and head home. But what happens when you meet someone who just seems like the perfect fit for you. When that person seem to sync with you on every wavelength and frequency. What would you do?

You feel your heart bursting out of your chest. You ask yourself is this real life or is it just fantasy (quote from Bohemian Rhapsody if you got that reference)? You felt like you've never connected with someone so deeply and emotionally before and you are just not sure what to make of these intense feelings.

You talk on the phone for hours without running out of things to say. He or she is able to guess your next sentence as if they were reading your mind. And you feel like you've been searching your whole life for this person. Going through guy after guy, or girl after girl, sifting through the noise, and this golden gem has finally presented itself to you.

In today's topic we will go through XX ways that you can do to move forward. Tips on how you can navigate that path forward and make a relationship that lasts a lifetime.

1.   Embrace These Feelings

Having butterflies in your stomach or feeling like your heart is overflowing could be signs that you are fully attracted to this person that you've found in your life. They have got your undivided attention and there is no one else that you are thinking of but him or her. Embrace these feelings. Accept that they are there to point a path to you. That you feel these things for a reason. Don't try to brush them aside or hide it under a mat thinking ignorance is bliss. As humans we are feeling creatures, so take these emotions and use them to your advantage.

2.   Don't Rush Things

When we like someone a lot, it can be easy for us to get caught up in the moment. We want to see the person every single day and we obsess over their texts and calls. Stop and take a breather. If you want a long-lasting relationship with this person, take things slow. There is no incentive for you to rush things if you foresee a long future ahead. Resist the urge to expect that the person will reciprocate the same intensity at the beginning phases of your relationship. Instead take it one step at a time. Don't rush into bed. Dating takes time.

3.   Always Be Yourself

It is easy for us to want to present the best front of ourselves when we are trying to woo the other person that we really like. We may change what we say or do to accommodate the other person because we want them to like us. But if we take it too far, we may lose our sense of identity in the process. Always make sure that you stay true to yourself. The other party has to like you for you, and not who you pretend to be. If that person is right for you, he or she will accept you for who you are and all the quirks that you may bring to the table.

4.   Stay Committed To Other Areas of Your Life

Obsessing over someone can become a bad habit for us if we are not mindful of our thoughts and actions. We may have a tendency to prioritise all the time and energy into that person while forgoing all the things we know we should be doing. We lose focus at work, is disinterested in family time, and we may even neglect our friends in the process. Always remember that those are the pillars of your life and to not waver in your commitment to them even though someone new and amazing has entered into your life.

5. Give The Person Time To Warm Up To You

We may feel strongly for the person, but it doesn't necessarily mean that they feel the exact same way about us right away. Building a relationship takes time, and we need to be mindful that things don't simply blossom overnight. A plant takes constant watering and sunlight to flower, and the same goes for courting and dating. Let the person see who you are gradually. Show them a different page of your book to them over time and let them enjoy you from cover to cover rather than giving them a spark-notes summary.

6. Go On Regular Dates

A good way to mesh your two lives together is to go on regular dates. Express little nuggets of interest to them every time you hang out. That way you are releasing some of that built up feelings you have inside you a little at a time. The last thing you want to do is scare the other person away by being too intense and overwhelming. Spending time together is a good way to also see if you are compatible and a good fit for each another.

7. Find New Things To Do Together

Finding new places to hang out, new things to eat, and new things to do, keeps things fresh between the two of you. That way you get to experience what that person is like in different places and settings. You may pick up more on their likes and dislikes that way. Don't forget to take things slow even though you are trying new things together.

8. Take It To The Next Level

If you feel like you've reached a point where you are certain that you like this person, and that he or she feels the same way about you, it may be time to take things to the next level. However long this process takes, ensure that both of you are on the same page. The last thing you want to do is face a rejection or ask too prematurely. Let things happen naturally, that way there is no second guessing.

Conclusion

Managing your feelings for someone you like a lot can be a tricky thing, but hopefully these tips will help you navigate through it all. I sincerely hope that you are able to build a life-long relationship with this treasured person as well. Life is too short to let good people slip by us.